R. W. Emerson.

Ralph Waldo Emerson
(1803–1882)

QUOTATIONS
OF
Ralph Waldo Emerson

APPLEWOOD BOOKS
Carlisle, Massachusetts

Copyright © 2018 Applewood Books, Inc.

Collected and edited by Camille Arbogast

Ralph Waldo Emerson portrait courtesy of the Library of Congress

Cover wallpaper image: Photographed from Emerson's Study at the Concord Museum, Concord, Massachusetts

Thank you for purchasing an Applewood book. Applewood reprints America's lively classics — books from the past that are still of interest to modern readers. For a free copy of our current catalog, please write or visit us at Applewood Books, 1 River Road, Carlisle, Massachusetts 01741.

www.awb.com

978-1-4290-9491-7

2 3 4 5 6 7 8 9 10

Ralph Waldo Emerson

RALPH WALDO EMERSON was born in Boston, Massachusetts, on May 25, 1803, to Ruth Haskins and William Emerson. His father, a minister, died when Emerson was eight. Emerson and his four brothers were raised by their mother with help from extended family.

Emerson entered Harvard College at fourteen. At college he began keeping a journal, which became a lifelong practice, leading to many of the themes on which he later wrote essays.

After teaching for a few years, Emerson attended Harvard Divinity School. He was ordained in 1829 and accepted a position as the pastor of Boston's Second Church. That year he also married Ellen Tucker, who died of tuberculosis only two years later in 1831. Devastated by her death, Emerson questioned his career, as well as some of the traditions of his church. He resigned his pulpit in late 1832 and left on a nine-month journey through Europe.

Upon his return to Massachusetts, he started a new career as a secular public speaker. He then met Lydia Jackson, later known as Lidian, and married her in 1835. They had four children: Waldo, Ellen, Edith, and Edward. The death of Waldo at the age of five was one of the great losses of Emerson's life. Emerson was also affected by the early deaths of two of his brothers.

The Emersons settled in Concord, Massachusetts. In Concord, Emerson encouraged the development of a community of writers and philosophers, which included Nathaniel Hawthorne and Henry David Thoreau.

In 1836, Emerson published *Nature*, considered a major work of American Transcendentalism. Two years later, he gave a controversial address to the graduating class of Harvard Divinity School students. These early works, along with essays such as "Self Reliance" (1841), earned Emerson a reputation as a radical new thinker. From 1842 to 1844, Emerson edited the Transcendentalist magazine *The Dial*.

In the 1850s, Emerson released *Representative Men* (1850) and *English Traits* (1856). Now a literary celebrity known as the "Sage of Concord," he was in demand as a speaker. Emerson also occasionally supported political causes, including publicly protesting the Fugitive Slave Act.

In the 1860s and 1870s, Emerson continued to publish well-received essay collections, releasing *Conduct of Life* in 1860, *Society and Solitude* in 1870, and *Letters and Social Aims* in 1876. Experiencing memory problems, in the 1870s he largely withdrew from public speaking.

Emerson died in Concord on April 27, 1882, and was buried in Concord's Sleepy Hollow Cemetery. He is considered one of the most influential American writers of the nineteenth century.

Quotations

of

Ralph Waldo Emerson

Can you believe, Waldo Emerson, that you may relieve yourself of this perpetual perplexity of choosing? & by putting your ear close to the soul, learn always the true way.

– Journal, New Bedford, Massachusetts, February 12, 1834

Lean without fear on your own tastes.

– Journal, Newton, Massachusetts, September 13, 1834

The domestic man loves no music so well as his kitchen clock and the airs which the logs sing to him as they burn in the fire-place.

– Journal, 1834

It is very easy in the world to live by the opinion of the world. It is very easy in solitude to be self-centered. But the finished man is he who in the midst of the crowd keeps with perfect sweetness the independence of solitude.

– Journal, December 21, 1834

I obey my highest impulses in declaring to you the feeling of deep and tender respect which you have inspired me.... Can I resist the impulse to beseech you to love me?... I have immense desire that you should love me, and that I might live with you alway.... And think it not strange, as you will not, that I write rather than speak. In the gravest acts of my life I more willingly trust my pen than my tongue.

– Proposal letter to Lydia Jackson, Concord, Massachusetts, January 24, 1835

I am born a poet, of a low class without doubt yet a poet. That is my nature & vocation. My singing be sure is very "husky" & is for the most part in prose. Still I am a poet in the sense of a perceiver & dear lover of the harmonies that are in the soul & in matter, & specially of the correspondences between these & those.

– Letter to his fiancée, Lydia Jackson, Concord, Massachusetts, February 1, 1835

The life of this world has but a limited worth in my eyes & really is not worth such a price as the toleration of slavery.

– Journal, February 2, 1835

I will read & write. Why not? All the snow is shovelled away, all the corn planted & the children & the creatures on the planet taken care of without my help. But if I do not read nobody will.

– Journal, March 27, 1835

Our age is retrospective. It builds the sepulchers of the fathers. It writes biographies, histories, and criticism. The foregoing generation beheld God and nature face to face; we, through their eyes. Why should not we also enjoy an original relation to the universe? Why should we not have a poetry and philosophy of insight and not of tradition, and a religion by revelation to us, and not the history of theirs?

– *Nature*, 1836

To go into solitude, a man needs to retire as much from his chamber as from society. I am not solitary whilst I read and write, though nobody is with me. But if a man would be alone, let him look at the stars.

– *Nature*, 1836

The lover of nature is he whose inward and outward senses are still truly adjusted to each other; who has retained the spirit of infancy even into the era of manhood. His intercourse with heaven and earth, becomes part of his daily food.
– *Nature*, 1836

I become a transparent eye-ball; I am nothing; I see all; the currents of the Universal Being circulate through me; I am part or particle of God.
– *Nature*, 1836

Every spirit builds itself a house, and beyond its house a world, and beyond its world a heaven. Know then, that the world exists for you. For you is the phenomenon perfect. What we are, that only can we see.... Build, therefore, your own world.
– *Nature*, 1836

I was made a hermit & am content with my lot. I pluck golden fruit from rare meetings with wise men. I can well abide alone in the intervals, and the fruit of my own tree shall have a better flavor.
– Journal, 1837

By the rude bridge that arched the flood,
Their flag to April's breeze unfurled,
There once the embattled farmers stood,
And fired the shot heard round the world.

– Hymn sung at the completion of the Concord Monument, Concord, Massachusetts, July 4, 1837

Abide by your spontaneous impression with good humoured inflexibility then most when the whole cry of voices is on the other side. Else, tomorrow a stranger will say with masterly good sense precisely what you have thought & felt all the time, & you will be forced to take with shame your own opinion from another.

– Journal, July 21, 1837

Meek young men grow up in libraries, believing it their duty to accept the views, which Cicero, which Locke, which Bacon, have given, forgetful that Cicero, Locke, and Bacon were only young men in libraries, when they wrote those books.

– "The American Scholar," an oration delivered before the Phi Beta Kappa Society, Cambridge, Massachusetts, August 31, 1837

There is then creative reading as well as creative writing. When the mind is braced by labor and invention, the page of whatever book we read becomes luminous with manifold allusion. Every sentence is doubly significant, and the sense of our author is as broad as the world.

– "The American Scholar," an oration delivered before the Phi Beta Kappa Society, Cambridge, Massachusetts, August 31, 1837

I stir in it for the sad reason that no other mortal will move & if I do not, why it is left undone. The amount of it, be sure, is merely a Scream but sometimes a scream is better than a thesis.

– Journal, April 23, 1838, on writing to President Van Buren to protest the removal of the Cherokee from the state of Georgia

Let me admonish you, to go alone: to refuse the good models, even those which are sacred to the imagination of men, and dare to love God without mediator or veil.

– "The Divinity School Address," Divinity College, Cambridge, Massachusetts, July 15, 1838

If utterance is denied, the thought lies like a burden on the man.

– "The Divinity School Address," Divinity College, Cambridge, Massachusetts, July 15, 1838

Imitation cannot go above its model. The imitator dooms himself to hopeless mediocrity.

– "The Divinity School Address," Divinity College, Cambridge, Massachusetts, July 15, 1838

The youth, intoxicated with his admiration of a hero, fails to see, that it is only a projection of his own soul, which he admires.

– "Literary Ethics," an oration delivered before the Literary Societies of Dartmouth College, Hanover, New Hampshire, July 24, 1838

Explore, and explore. Be neither chided nor flattered out of your position of perpetual inquiry. Neither dogmatize yourself, nor accept another's dogmatism. Why should you renounce your right to traverse the star-lit deserts of truth, for the premature comforts of an acre, house, and barn? Truth also has its roof, and bed, and board.

– "Literary Ethics," an oration delivered before the Literary Societies of Dartmouth College, Hanover, New Hampshire, July 24, 1838

Two persons lately, children of the most wise God, have admonished me by their silent being. It seemed as if each answered to my heart's inquiry, Whence is your power? "From my nonconformity. I never listened to your people's law, or to what they call their gospel, & wasted my time. I was content with the simple rural poverty of my own. Hence this sweetness."

– Journal, 1841

Can anything be so elegant as to have few wants and to serve them one's self?

– "Man the Reformer," a lecture read before the Mechanics' Apprentices' Library Association, Boston, Massachusetts, January 25, 1841

There is one mind common to all individual men. Every man is an inlet to the same and to all of the same.

– "History," *Essays: First Series*, 1841

The creation of a thousand forests is in one acorn.
– "History," *Essays: First Series*, 1841

Every revolution was first a thought in one man's mind, and when the same thought occurs to another man, it is the key to that era.
– "History," *Essays: First Series*, 1841

All history becomes subjective; in other words, there is properly no history, only biography. Every mind must know the whole lesson for itself, must go over the whole ground. What it does not see, what it does not live, it will not know.
– "History," *Essays: First Series*, 1841

To believe your own thought, to believe that what is true for you in your private heart is true for all men,—that is genius.
– "Self-Reliance," *Essays: First Series*, 1841

There is a time in every man's education when he arrives at the conviction that envy is ignorance; that imitation is suicide; that he must take himself for better or for worse as his portion; that though the wide universe is full of good, no kernel of nourishing corn can come to him but through his toil bestowed on that plot of ground which is given to him to till.

– "Self-Reliance," *Essays: First Series*, 1841

Trust thyself: every heart vibrates to that iron string.

– "Self-Reliance," *Essays: First Series*, 1841

Society everywhere is in conspiracy against the manhood of every one of its members. Society is a joint-stock company, in which the members agree, for the better securing of his bread to each shareholder, to surrender the liberty and culture of the eater.

– "Self-Reliance," *Essays: First Series*, 1841

Whoso would be a man must be a non-conformist.

– "Self-Reliance," *Essays: First Series*, 1841

Nothing is at last sacred but the integrity of your own mind.

– "Self-Reliance," *Essays: First Series*, 1841

A foolish consistency is the hobgoblin of little minds, adored by little statesmen and philosophers and divines.

– "Self-Reliance," *Essays: First Series*, 1841

I like the silent church before the service begins, better than any preaching.

– "Self-Reliance," *Essays: First Series*, 1841

I shall endeavour to nourish my parents, to support my family, to be the chaste husband of one wife,— but these relations I must fill after a new and unprecedented way. I appeal from your customs. I must be myself. I cannot break myself any longer for you, or you.

– "Self-Reliance," *Essays: First Series*, 1841

Insist on yourself; never imitate.

– "Self-Reliance," *Essays: First Series*, 1841

Nothing can bring you peace but yourself. Nothing can bring you peace but the triumph of principles.

– "Self-Reliance," *Essays: First Series*, 1841

If you would not be known to do any thing, never do it.

– "Self-Reliance," *Essays: First Series*, 1841

The epochs of our life are not in the visible facts of our choice of a calling, our marriage, our acquisition of an office, and the like, but in a silent thought by the wayside as we walk; in a thought which reverses our entire manner of life, and says,—"Thus has thou done, but it were better thus."

– "Spiritual Laws," *Essays: First Series*, 1841

We know that the ancestor of every action is a thought.

– "Spiritual Laws," *Essays: First Series*, 1841

All mankind love a lover.

– "Love," *Essays: First Series*, 1841

I do not wish to treat friendship daintily, but with roughest courage. When they are real, they are not glass threads or frostwork, but the solidest thing we know.

– "Friendship," *Essays: First Series*, 1841

The only reward of virtue is virtue; the only way to have a friend is to be one.

– "Friendship," *Essays: First Series*, 1841

In skating over thin ice, our safety is in our speed.

– "Prudence," *Essays: First Series*, 1841

Life wastes itself whilst we are preparing to live.

– "Prudence," *Essays: First Series*, 1841

It was a high counsel that I once heard given to a young person,—"Always do what you are afraid to do."

– "Heroism," *Essays: First Series*, 1841

Our life is an apprenticeship to the truth, that around every circle another can be drawn; that there is no end in nature, that every end is a beginning; that there is always another dawn risen on mid-noon, and under every deep a lower deep opens.

– "Circles," *Essays: First Series*, 1841

People wish to be settled; only as far as they are unsettled is there any hope for them.

– "Circles," *Essays: First Series*, 1841

Nothing great was ever achieved without enthusiasm. The way of life is wonderful: it is by abandonment.

– "Circles," *Essays: First Series*, 1841

We do not determine what we will think. We only open our senses, clear away as we can all obstruction from the fact, and suffer the intellect to see. We have little control over our thoughts. We are the prisoners of ideas.

– "Intellect," *Essays: First Series*, 1841

Though we travel the world over to find the beautiful, we must carry it with us, or we find it not.

– "Art," *Essays: First Series*, 1841

Nothing astonishes men so much as common-sense and plain dealing.

– "Art," *Essays: First Series*, 1841

I would have my book read as I have read my favorite books not with explosion & astonishment, a marvel and a rocket, but a friendly & agreeable influence stealing like the scent of a flower or the sight of a new landscape on a traveller.

– Journal, 1841

Do not be too timid & squeamish about your actions. All life is an experiment. The more experiments you make, the better.

– Journal, 1842

We fancy that men are individuals; but every pumpkin in the field goes through every point of pumpkin history.

– Journal, 1844

Money is of no value; it cannot spend itself. All depends on the skill of the spender.

– "The Young American," a lecture read to the Mercantile Library Association, Boston, Massachusetts, February 7, 1844

Society gains nothing whilst a man, not himself renovated, attempts to renovate things around him.

– "New England Reformers," lecture given at Amory Hall, Boston, Massachusetts, March 3, 1844

Is not every man sometimes a radical in politics? Men are conservatives when they are least vigorous, or when they are most luxurious. They are conservatives after dinner, or before taking their rest; when they are sick, or aged; in the morning, or when their intellect or their conscience has been aroused; when they hear music, or when they read poetry, they are radicals.

– "New England Reformers," lecture given at Amory Hall, Boston, Massachusetts, March 3, 1844

The reward of a thing well done, is to have done it.

– "New England Reformers," lecture given at Amory Hall, Boston, Massachusetts, March 3, 1844

We do not know today whether we are busy or idle. In times when we thought ourselves indolent, we have afterwards discovered, that much was accomplished, and much begun in us.

– "Experience," *Essays: Second Series*, 1844

To finish the moment, to find the journey's end in every step of the road, to live the greatest number of good hours, is wisdom.
– "Experience," *Essays: Second Series*, 1844

The wise through excess of wisdom is made a fool.
– "Experience," *Essays: Second Series*, 1844

The years teach much which the days never know.
– "Experience," *Essays: Second Series*, 1844

Good men must not obey the laws too well.
– "Politics," *Essays: Second Series*, 1844

O day of days, when we can read! The reader and the book. Either without the other is naught.
– Journal, 1847

An artist spends himself, like the crayon in his hand, till he is all gone.

– Journal, 1848

Like the New England soil, my talent is good only whilst I work it.

– Journal, 1849

Every hero becomes a bore at last.

– "Uses of Great Men," *Representative Men*, 1850

Every book is a quotation; and every house is a quotation out of all forests and mines and stone quarries; and every man is a quotation from all his ancestors.

– "Plato; or, The Philosopher," *Representative Men*, 1850

Great geniuses have the shortest biographies. Their cousins can tell you nothing about them. They lived in their writings, and so their house and street life was trivial and commonplace.

– "Plato; or, The Philosopher," *Representative Men*, 1850

Our life is March weather, savage and serene in one hour.

– "Montaigne; or the Skeptic," *Representative Men*, 1850

Talent alone cannot make a writer. There must be a man behind the book.

– "Goethe: or the Writer," *Representative Men*, 1850

If our resistance to this law is not right, there is no right. This is not meddling with other people's affairs: this is hindering other people from meddling with us.

– "The Fugitive Slave Law," an address to citizens of Concord, Massachusetts, May 3, 1851

I trust a good deal to common fame, as we all must. If a man has good corn, or wood, or boards, or pigs, to sell, or can make better chairs or knives, crucibles or church organs, than anybody else, you will find a broad hard-beaten road to his house, though it be in the woods.

– Journal, 1855

I think we must get rid of slavery, or we must get rid of freedom.

– "The Assault upon Mr. Sumner," speech read at a meeting at Town Hall, Concord, Massachusetts, May 26, 1856

The Frenchman invented the ruffle; the Englishman added the shirt.

– "Ability," *English Traits*, 1856

So far as a man thinks, he is free.

– "Fate," *Conduct of Life*, 1860

There is no way to success in our art, but to take off your coat, grind paint, and work like a digger on the railroad, all day and every day.

– "Power," *Conduct of Life*, 1860

The socialism of our day has done good service in setting men to thinking how certain civilizing benefits, now only enjoyed by the opulent, can be enjoyed by all.

– "Wealth," *Conduct of Life*, 1860

Art is a jealous mistress, and, if a man have a genius for painting, poetry, music, architecture, or philosophy, he makes a bad husband, and an ill provider, and should be wise in season, and not fetter himself with duties which will embitter his days, and spoil him for his proper work.

– "Wealth," *Conduct of Life*,1860

We say the cows laid out Boston. Well, there are worse surveyors.

– "Wealth," *Conduct of Life*,1860

Manners are very communicable: men catch them from each other.

– "Behavior," *Conduct of Life*, 1860

Our chief want in life, is, somebody who shall make us do what we can.

– "Considerations by the Way," *Conduct of Life*,1860

Make yourself necessary to somebody. Do not make life hard to any.

– "Considerations by the Way," *Conduct of Life*, 1860

In this national crisis, it is not argument that we want, but that rare courage which dares commit itself to a principle.

– "American Civilization," lecture given at the Smithsonian Institution, Washington, D.C., January 31, 1862

He declined to give up his large ambition of knowledge and action for any narrow craft or profession, aiming at a much more comprehensive calling, the art of living well.

– "On Thoreau," eulogy for Henry David Thoreau, delivered at First Parish Church, Concord, Massachusetts, May 7, 1862

This middle-class country had got a middle-class president, at last.

– "Abraham Lincoln," remarks at funeral services for President Lincoln held in Concord, Massachusetts, April 19, 1865

Poetry teaches the enormous force of a few words, & in proportion to the inspiration, checks loquacity.

– Journal, 1866

Hitch your wagon to a star.

– "Civilization," *Society and Solitude*, 1870

The ornament of a house is the friends who frequent it.

– "Domestic Life," *Society and Solitude*, 1870

I should as soon think of swimming across Charles River when I wish to go to Boston, as of reading all my books in originals when I have them rendered for me in my mother tongue.

– "Books," *Society and Solitude*, 1870

'Tis the good reader that makes the good book; a good head cannot read amiss, in every book he finds passages which seem confidences or asides hidden from all else and unmistakably meant for his ear.

– "Success," *Society and Solitude*, 1870

Tobacco, coffee, alcohol, hashish, prussic acid, strychnine are weak dilutions: the surest poison is time.

– "Old Age," *Society and Solitude*, 1870

We postpone our literary work until we have more ripeness and skill to write, and we one day discover that our literary talent was a youthful effervescence which we have now lost.

– "Old Age," *Society and Solitude*, 1870

Skill to do comes of doing; knowledge comes by eyes always open, and working hands; and there is no knowledge that is not power.

– "Old Age," *Society and Solitude*, 1870

By necessity, by proclivity and by delight, we all quote.

– "Quotation and Originality," *Letters and Social Aims*, 1876

R. W. Emerson.